Once upon a time there was a lady.

The lady had a beautiful heart.

She was growing a baby inside her
and the sun shone brightly upon them.

One day, out of the blue,
her heart was broken into tiny pieces

and the sun disappeared.

She tried to mend her heart
with family and friends and sticky tape

but one piece was missing.

So the cloud stayed put

and her heart worked well enough.

Soon the baby arrived

And the lady's heart doubled in size.

The lady worried about the cloud.

It often rained.

She worried it would rain on her baby

and make the baby sad too.

The lady and her baby grew together.

They played together.

They explored together.

They snuggled together.

Despite the rain

it was a magical world, full of wonder.

As the baby girl grew

she shone brighter and brighter.

The cloud still rained sometimes

but the little girl was sunshine.

And so together

they made a rainbow.

www.ingramcontent.com/pod-product-compliance
Ingram Content Group UK Ltd.
Pitfield, Milton Keynes, MK11 3LW, UK
UKHW060102300726
14090UKWH00003B/351

9781979513012